Instant XenMobile MDM

A guide to effectively equipping mobile devices with configuration, security, provisioning, and support capabilities using XenMobile, the world's most popular mobile management software

Aamir Lakhani

BIRMINGHAM - MUMBAI

Instant XenMobile MDM

First published: September 2013

Production Reference: 1230913

Published by Packt Publishing Ltd.
Livery Place
35 Livery Street
Birmingham B3 2PB, UK.

ISBN 978-1-84969-626-5

www.packtpub.com

Credits

Author

Aamir Lakhani

Reviewers

Joseph Muniz

Eran Kinsbruner

Acquisition Editor

Anthony Albuquerque

Commissioning Editor

Amit Ghodake

Technical Editor

Krishnaveni Haridas

Project Coordinator

Romal Karani

Proofreader

Linda Morris

Production Coordinator

Nilesh R. Mohite

Cover Work

Nilesh R. Mohite

Cover Image

Aditi Gajjar

About the Author

Aamir Lakhani is a leading cyber security and cyber counter intelligence architect for World Wide Technology, Inc. (WWT). He is responsible for WWT's efforts to provide IT security solutions to major commercial and federal enterprise organizations.

He leads projects that implement security postures for Fortune 500 companies, the United States Department of Defense, major healthcare providers, educational institutions, and financial and media organizations. He has designed offensive counter defense measures for defense and intelligence agencies, and has assisted organizations in defending themselves from active strike-back attacks perpetrated by underground cyber groups. He is considered an industry leader in support of detailed architectural engagements and projects on topics related to cyber defense, mobile application threats, malware and Advanced Persistent Threat (APT) research, and Dark Security. He is the author of the soon to be released book Ultimate Web Penetration Testing with Kali Linux, in conjunction with Packt Publishing.

Writing under the pseudonym Dr. Chaos, he also operates the DrChaos.com blog. In its recent list of 46 Federal Technology Experts to Follow on Twitter, Forbes magazine described him as "a blogger, infosec specialist, super hero...and all round good guy."

I would like to thank my parents, Mahmood and Nasreen Lakhani. Thank you for always encouraging me, pushing me to be my best, and nourishing my hunger for knowledge. I would also like thank my sisters, Noureen and Zahra who have always been there for me and are my best friends. Last, but definitely not least I would like to thank my team and colleagues at World Wide Technology, Inc. for mentoring me and giving me the ability to do what I love. It is easy to see why WWT is one of the best places to work, it's the people, management, and attitude.

About the Reviewers

Eran Kinsbruner is the director of product marketing at Perfecto Mobile, one of the leading mobile cloud and automation companies. Formerly CTO for mobile testing and Texas Instruments project manager at Matrix. He has been in testing since 1999 with experience that includes managing teams at Qulicke & Soffa, Sun Microsystems, General Electric, and NeuStar. The co-inventor of a test exclusion automated mechanism for mobile J2ME testing at Sun Microsystems, he has experience in the mobile testing world and constantly presents in large conferences around subjects such as Quest, StarEast, STP, and TestKit. You can find Eran on Facebook, Twitter @ek121268, LinkedIn, and his professional mobile testing blogs at ek121268.wordpress.com and blog.perfectomobile.com. He works for Perfecto Mobile which is one of the leading mobile cloud companies, offering, based on its platform (the MobileCloud™), a wide range of mobile products and enterprise solutions such as Mobile Manual, Automation, Performance, and Monitoring testing for real devices such as Smartphones and Tablets. The company also provides integrations to leading market tools for continuous integration (for example, Jenkins), testing, and more. It is HP's chosen mobile testing solution, and with a joint effort between the two companies, they developed the UFT Mobile solution. He has published many bylines and articles such as Electronic Design, ToolsJournal, and APM Digest.

Joseph Muniz is a solutions architect and security researcher. He started his career in software development and later managed networks as a contracted technical resource. He moved into consulting and found a passion for security while meeting with a variety of customers. He has been involved with the design and implementation of multiple projects, ranging from Fortune 500 corporations to large federal networks. He runs the `http://TheSecurityBlogger.com` website, a popular resource regarding security and product implementation. You can also find him speaking at live events, as well as involved with other publications. Recent events include him being a speaker for "Social Media Deception" at the 2013 ASIS International conference, speaker for "Making Bring Your Own Device (BYOD) Work" at the Government Solutions Forum, Washington DC, Author of Web Penetration Testing with Kali Linux, Packt Publishing, August 2013 and article on "Compromising Passwords" in PenTest Magazine - Backtrack Compendium, July 2013. In his spare time, he can be found behind turntables scratching classic vinyl or on the soccer pitch hacking away at the local club teams.

I dedicate my involvement in this book to my charming little battle-axe of a wife Ning and hand grenade of happiness also known as my daughter Raylin.

www.packtpub.com

Support files, eBooks, discount offers and more

You might want to visit www.packtpub.com for support files and downloads related to your book.

Did you know that Packt offers eBook versions of every book published, with PDF and ePub files available? You can upgrade to the eBook version at www.packtpub.com and as a print book customer, you are entitled to a discount on the eBook copy. Get in touch with us at service@packtpub.com for more details.

At www.packtpub.com, you can also read a collection of free technical articles, sign up for a range of free newsletters and receive exclusive discounts and offers on Packt books and eBooks.

packtlib.packtpub.com

Do you need instant solutions to your IT questions? PacktLib is Packt's online digital book library. Here, you can access, read and search across Packt's entire library of books.

Why Subscribe?

- ✦ Fully searchable across every book published by Packt
- ✦ Copy and paste, print and bookmark content
- ✦ On demand and accessible via web browser

Free Access for Packt account holders

If you have an account with Packt at www.packtpub.com, you can use this to access PacktLib today and view nine entirely free books. Simply use your login credentials for immediate access.

Table of Contents

Instant XenMobile

Welcome to *Instant XenMobile*. This book will provide you with all the information that you need to get set up with XenMobile. You will learn the basics of XenMobile and how to deploy, secure, and manage mobile devices in your organization, and discover some tips and tricks for using XenMobile.

This book contains the following sections:

So, what is XenMobile? helps you to find out what XenMobile actually is, what you can do with it, and how it can help an organization to implement advanced mobile solutions.

Installation helps you to learn how to download and install XenMobile with minimum fuss and then set it up, so that you can quickly setup and use it in your organization.

Quick start – setting up XenMobile for the first time will show you how to perform one of the core tasks of XenMobile, that is creating courses. Follow the steps to create your own course, which will be the basis of most of your work in Moodle.

Top 6 features you need to know about helps you learn the most important features of XenMobile, which are as follows:

+ Reporting
+ Application stores
+ Secure Mail Gateway
+ The XenMobile service manager
+ Dashboard management
+ Common management tasks

By the end of this section, you will be able to manage the mobile devices in your organization using XenMobile.

People and places you should get to know provides you with many useful links to the project page and forums, as well as a number of helpful articles, tutorials, blogs, and the Twitter feeds of Moodle supercontributors (since, every mobility project is centered on a community)

So, what is XenMobile?

Reports from the Internet estimate that there will be an explosion of mobile devices in corporate businesses. Mobile devices are quickly becoming the computing device of choice. Unlike traditional computing devices, mobile devices are designed for consumers before businesses, and therefore organizations are having a difficult time securing and managing these devices. They have turned to mobile device management solutions to help them manage both corporate and BYOD devices in a secure manner within their organization.

XenMobile is the next generation of **mobile device management** (**MDM**) from Citrix. XenMobile provides organizations the ability to automate most of the administrative tasks on mobile devices for both corporate and highly secured environments. In addition, it can also help organizations in managing bring your own device (**BYOD**) environments.

XenMobile MDM allows administrators to configure role-based management for device provisioning and security for both corporate and employee-owned BYOD devices.

When a user enrolls with their mobile device, an organization can provision policies and apps to devices automatically, blacklist or whitelist apps, detect and protect against jail broken devices, and wipe or selectively wipe a device that is lost, stolen, or out of compliance. A selective wipe means that only corporate or sensitive data is deleted, but personal data stays intact on a user's device. XenMobile supports every major mobile OS that is being used today, giving users the freedom to choose and use a device of their choice.

Citrix has done an excellent job recognizing that organizations need MDM as a key component for a secure mobile ecosystem. Citrix XenMobile adds other features such as secure @WorkMail, @WorkWeb, and ShareFile integration, so that organizations can securely and safely access e-mail, the Internet, and exchange documents in a secure manner. There are other popular solutions on the market that have similar claims. Unlike other solutions, they rely on container-based solutions which limit native applications. Container-based solutions are applications that embed corporate data, e-mail, contact, and calendar data. Unfortunately, in many cases these solutions break the user experience by limiting how they can use native applications. XenMobile does this without compromising the user experience, allowing the secure applications to exist and share the same calendar, contact, and other key integration points on the mobile device. They were the only vendors at the time of writing this book, that had a single management platform which provided MDM features with secure storage, integrated VDI, multitenant, and application load balancing features, which we believe are some of the differentiators between XenMobile and its competitors.

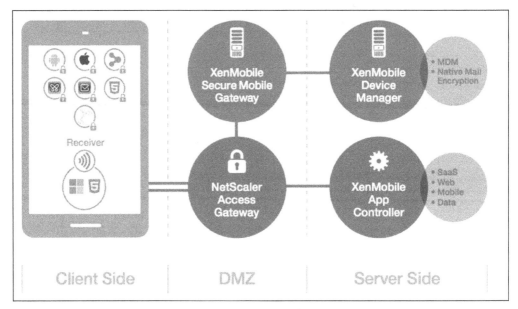

Citrix XenMobile MDM Architecture

Mobile application stores (MAS) and **mobile application management (MAN)** are the concepts which you manage and secure access to individual applications on a mobile device, but leave the rest of the mobile device unmanaged. In some scenarios, people consider this as a great way of managing BYOD environments because organizations only need to worry about the applications and the data they manage. XenMobile has support for mobile application management and supports individual application policies, in addition to the holistic device policies found on other competing products.

In this book, you will gain a deep understanding of XenMobile and its key features. You will learn how to install, configure, and use XenMobile in your environment to manage corporate and BYOD environments. We will then explore how to get started with XenMobile, configure policies and security, and how to deploy XenMobile in our organization. Next, we will look at some of the advanced features in XenMobile, how and when to use them, how to manage compliance breaches, and other top features. Finally, we will explore what do next when you have XenMobile configured.

Welcome to the world of XenMobile MDM. Let's get started.

Mobile device management (MDM) is a software solution that helps the organizations to manage, provision, and secure the lifecycle of a mobile device. MDM systems allow enterprises to mass deploy policies, settings, and applications to mobile devices. These features can include provisioning the mobile devices for Wi-Fi access, corporate e-mail, develop in-house applications, tracking locations, and remote wipe. Mobile device management solutions for enterprise corporations provide these capabilities over the air and for multiple mobile operating systems.

Blackberry can be considered as the world's first real mobile enterprise solution with their product **Blackberry Enterprise Server** (**BES**). BES is still considered as a very capable and well-respected MDM solution. Blackberry devices were one of the first devices that provided organizations an accurate control of their users' mobile devices. The Blackberry device was essentially a dumb device until it was connected to a BES server. Once connected to a BES server, the Blackberry device would download policies, which would govern what features the device could use. This included everything from voice roaming, Internet usage, and even camera and storage policies. Because of its detailed configurability, Blackberry devices became the standard for most corporations wanting to use mobile devices and securing them.

Apple and Google have made the smartphone a mainstream device and the tablet the computing platform of choice. People ended up waiting days in line to buy the latest gadget, and once they had it, you better believe they wanted to use it all the time. All of a sudden, organizations were getting hundreds of people wanting to connect their personal devices to the corporate network in order to work more efficiently with a device they enjoyed. The revolution of consumerization of IT had begun. In addition to Apple and Google devices, XenMobile supports Blackberry, Windows Phone, and other well-known mobile operating systems.

Many vendors rushed to bring solutions to organizations to help them manage their Apple and mobile devices in enterprise architectures. Vendors tried to give organizations the same management and security that Blackberry had provided them with previous BES features. Over the years, Apple and Google both recognized the need for mobile management and started building mobile device management features in their operating system, so that MDM solutions could provide better granular management and security control for enterprise organizations.

Today organizations are replacing older mobile devices in favor of Apple and Google devices. They feel comfortable in having these devices connected to corporate networks because they believe that they can manage them and secure them with MDM solutions. MDM solutions are the platform for organizations to ensure that mobile devices meet the technical, legal, and business compliance needed for their users to use devices of their choice, that are modern, and in many cases more productive than their legacy counterparts. MDM vendors have chosen to be container-based solutions, or device-based management. Container-based solutions provide segmentation of device data and allow organizations to completely ignore the rest of the device since all corporate data is self-contained. A good analogy for container-based solutions is Outlook Web Access. Outlook Web Access allows any computer to access Exchange email through a web browser. Computer software and applications are completely agnostic to corporate e-mail. Container-based solutions are similar, since they are indifferent to the mobile device data and other configuration components when being used to access an organization's resources, for example, e-mail on a mobile phone.

Device-based management solutions allow organizations to manage device and application settings, but can only enforce security policies based on the features made available to them by device manufacturers. XenMobile is a device-based management solution, however, it has many of the features found in container-based solutions giving organizations the best of both worlds.

Installation

In five easy steps, you can install and set up XenMobile on your system

Step 1 – what do I need?

Before you install XenMobile, you need to check whether you have all of the required elements, which are as follows:

 These values are updated as of August 2013. Please note that users should use the recommended values. The minimum values should only be used for lab environments with less than 10 mobile devices used for testing.

✦ **Disk space**: 500 MB free (min). However, most installations will require at least 10 GB free.

✦ **Memory**: 1 GB (min), 4 GB (recommended). The server must use an Intel Xeon class running at 3Ghz or AMD Opteron 1.8 Ghz class or faster processor.

✦ Moodle requires a web server environment and it runs in Apache and IIS easily. Moodle should run in any server environment that supports PHP.

✦ Server must be physical or virtual. We have tested this extensively on both the VMware ESXi and VMWarevCloud environments, along with Microsoft Hyper-V environments and it did not have any issue with virtual platforms.

✦ You must ensure that you do not have any other software installed and running, including web servers, database servers, or other server type software running on XenMobile. The system should be purposefully built only for Citrix.

✦ XenMobile will install PostgreSQL, however other SQL servers can be used. For large installations an external SQL server is recommended.

Step 2 – obtaining XenMobile software

If you want to download the XenMobile MDM you need to contact Citrix to get a demo of the software. Citrix offers cloud-based demos, you can even request to download their software at: http://deliver.citrix.com/XenMobileMDM.html/.

We would suggest that anyone who is interested in XenMobile requests the cloud-based demo. These requests usually come from IT teams or the office of the CIO in an organization. It has all the features of the on-premise demo, but does not require you to set up or install the system. All the features can be tested and experienced with the cloud-based demo.

Step 3 – Java requirements

In addition to the hardware requirements described in the first step, most of the installations will need their Java software updated on their systems. XenMobile requires the following Java components before the installation of the XenMobile software:

- ✦ Oracle Java SE 7 JDK (JDK download edition) update 11 and higher
- ✦ **Java Cryptography Extension** (**JCE**) unlimited strength jurisdiction policy files 7

From your XenMobile server, go to `http://www.oracle.com/technetwork/java/javase/downloads/java-archive-downloads-javase7-521261.html#jdk-7u4-oth-JPR` to download Java. You may be asked to register on the Java's website before you are allowed to download the file. Please note, that the Java versions are very specific. You should check with the Citrix XenMobile documentation to check if updates to the versions of Java have occurred since the time of writing. The registration page is as follows:

The Java download registration Page

Once Java is downloaded, simply double-click the installation file on the XenMobile server to install it, as shown in the following screenshot:

The Java installation file

After you download the Java file, you must additionally download JCE. The following is the link to Oracle's web page from where you can download the additional Java components needed to install XenMobile:

http://www.oracle.com/technetwork/java/javase/downloads/jce-7-download-432124.html

The following page opens up:

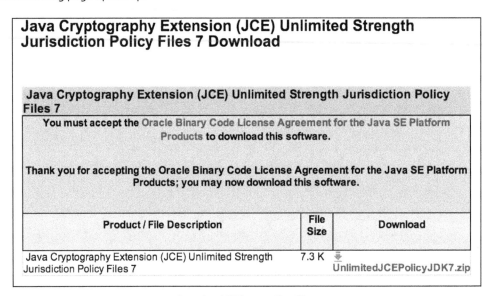

Download JCE encryption files

After you download and extract the JCE package, copy the `local_policy.jar` and `US_export_policy.jar` files to the `<java-home>\jre\lib\security` folder and overwrite the existing files. This means that on most of the systems you will replace the files in the `C:\Program Files\Java\jre7\lib\security` directory.

You can see from the following screenshot that we are moving the files from the downloaded and extracted archive into our Java home directory. Select **Move and Replace** when prompted:

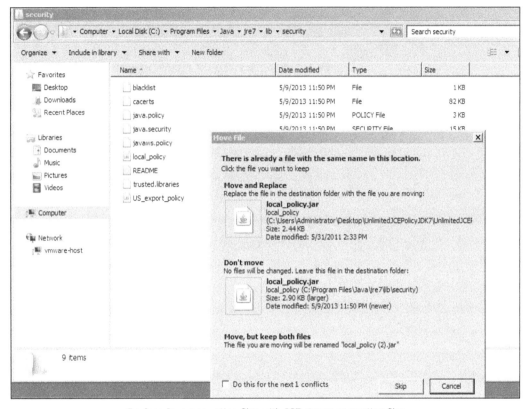

Replace Java encryption files with JCE strong encryption files

Step 4 – installing XenMobile

You are now ready to install the Citrix XenMobile software on our server. You will use the installation file that was sent to you from Citrix after you registered to obtain the software on step 2.You can install the software by performing the following steps:

1. Double-click on the installation file.

2. Click on **Next >** to continue with the installation, as shown in the following screenshot:

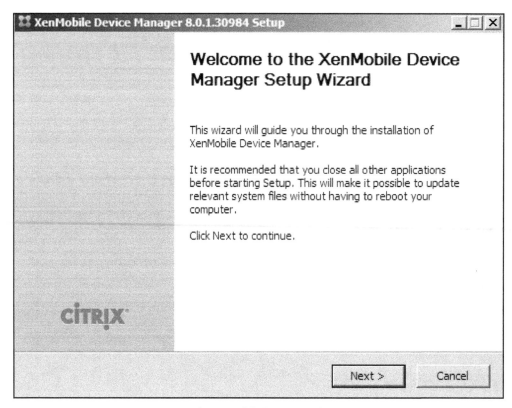

The XenMobile Setup wizard

✦ Click on **Next >** to install XenMobile **Database server** and XenMobile **Application server**. If you have your own database server, you may uncheck the **Database server** option:

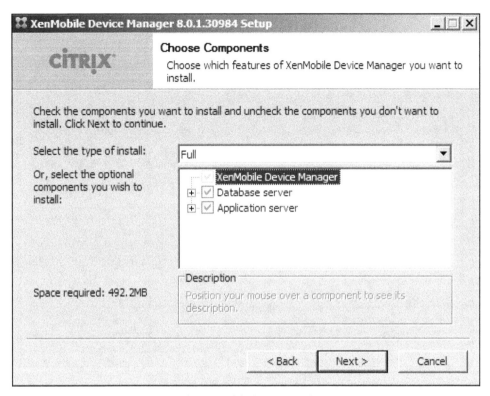

The XenMobile Setup Wizard

3. If you did not uncheck the installation of the database server, you will be asked to continue to install the PostgreSQL server, as shown in the following screenshot:

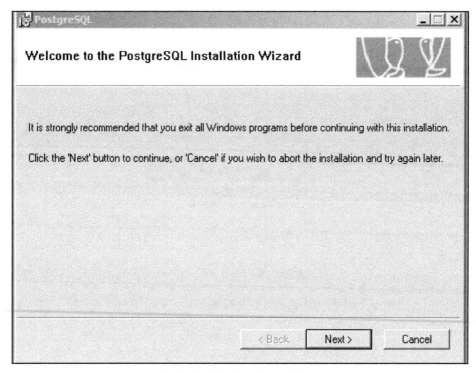

The PostgreSQL Installation Wizard

4. Review the default installation options. There is no need to change them. You may select additional options if you require them.

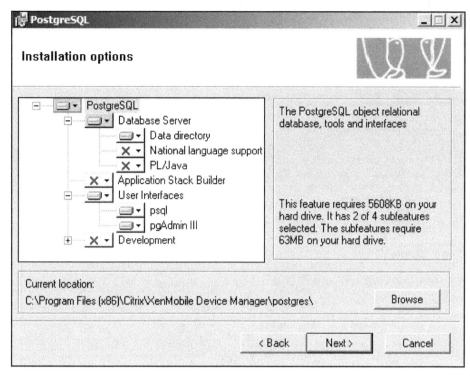

The PostgreSQL Installation Wizard

5. You will be prompted to create a user. Click on **Yes** to accept this message, as shown in the following screenshot:

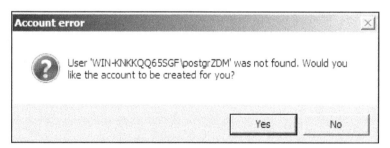

Creating ZDM database user

6. You will be asked for any additional components which you would like to install for the SQL server. You may select any additional components you may need, however XenMobile just needs the default components. You may click on **Next >** to continue, as shown in the following screenshot:

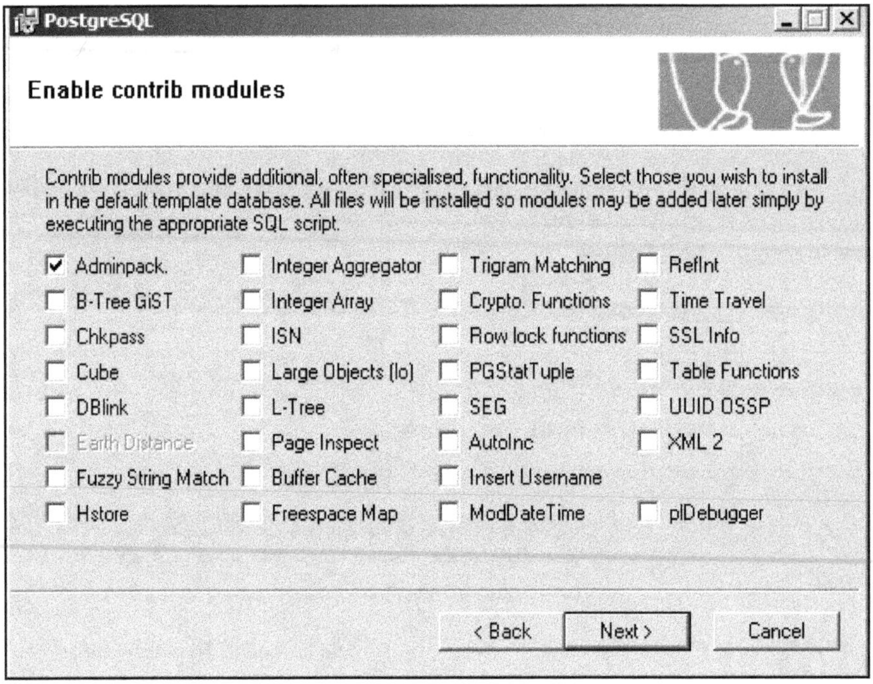

The additional database components

7. You need to add your licensed file for XenMobile that you received from Citrix at this point. If you do not have a licensed file you may simply click on **Next >,** as shown in the following screenshot:

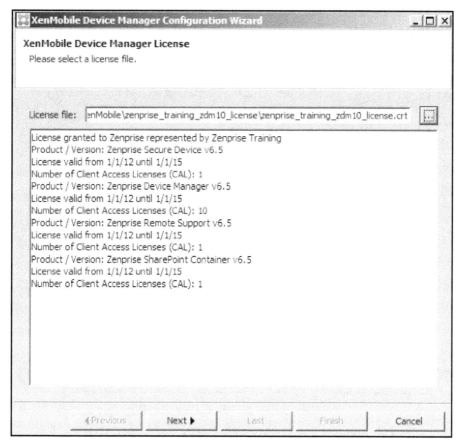

Citrix XenMobile licensing

8. You must enter the name of your XenMobile server. This name should be a fully qualified DNS name assigned to you by XenMobile. You need to make sure the name of the server is fully resolvable by an external DNS from the Internet.

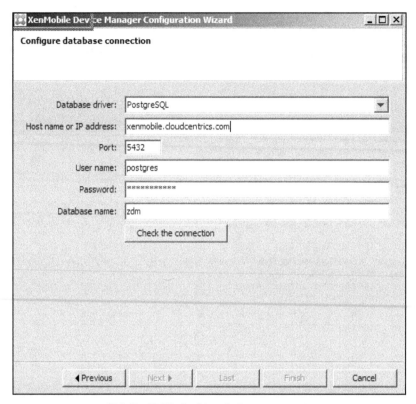

Citrix XenMobile final installation components

9. You need to enter your SQL server's admin username. If you used the default settings, the username will be `postgres`. Please note, that you do not have to use this as the password, you can choose any password you like.

10. You also need to enter your password that you set yourself earlier during the installation.

11. You will be asked to accept the name of the database. The default name is ZDM. You should not change this name. You must keep the default name of the database as ZDM.

12. Click on **Continue**. The installation can take up to 15 minutes to complete.

Step 5 – rebooting your server

Once your server is rebooted, ensure you do not have any errors appearing on the screen. XenMobile can take up to 5 minutes after the server is started for the application to get fully loaded, so be patient.

And that's it

By this time, you should have a working installation of XenMobile MDM and should be free to play around and discover more about it. Open up a web browser (all the major web browsers that support Java Version 7 will work) and go to: `https://localhost/zdm`. You will be taken to the following screenshot:

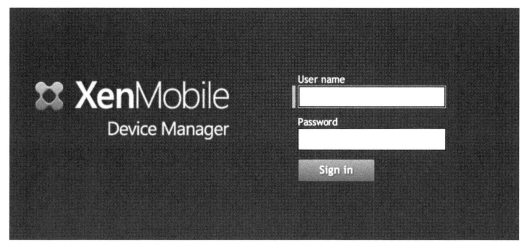

The XenMobile MDM's login screen

Quick start – setting up your XenMobile server

A mobile device policy is something which your organization can use to manage mobile devices. Policies can be used to distinguish mobile devices between corporate and BYOD devices. They can be used to automate the provisioning of devices into an organization and assign security policies. Before you can configure policies, you must configure your XenMobile server with basic configuration settings. In this section, we will show you how to configure XenMobile.

Step 1 – setting up XenMobile for the first time

When you log in to XenMobile for the first time, you will open up a browser and go to `https://server_ip_address/zdm`. You will enter the username and password you had set during the initial installation. Once you log in, you are presented with a dashboard with a quick view of your system, as shown in the following screenshot:

The dashboard

Don't worry if this looks empty, we will soon enroll devices and start configuring policies. As we enroll devices, our dashboard will start displaying more relevant information.

Step 2 – setting up server options

Select the **Option** button on the top-right side of the screen. This will bring up the server options page, as shown in the following screenshot. This is where we will enter the basic server and administrative information for our XenMobile server as follows:

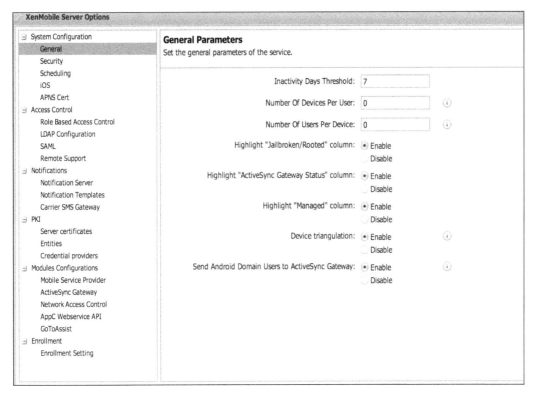

Server options

Initial parameters are default, but they can easily be changed based on the needs of an organization. Most options are self-explanatory, however, we will cover the more popular and complex options in further steps.

Step 3 – blocking jailbroken and rooted devices

Apple iOS devices or Google android devices can be jailbroken or rooted. Jailbreaking or rooting a device gives users access to settings and lets them install applications that have not been approved by the manufacturers. This may include Internet tethering applications to allow users to use their devices as mobile modems, tweaking voice settings, or installing applications that are only available in different countries.

Many threats by mobile devices on iOS and Android platforms are caused by software that requires the system to be rooted (Android) or jailbroken (iOS). Rooted and jailbroken applications do not go through the same verification process as normal applications. XenMobile can detect if these devices violate compliance and block them from accessing corporate applications and other resources. The configurations options are shown in the following screenshot:

Always Add Device:	○ Enable
	◉ Disable
Block Rooted Android and Jailbroken iOS Enrollment:	○ Enable
	◉ Disable
8 Char Strong ID:	◉ Enable
	○ Disable

Blocking Jailbroken and Rooted devices

These options allow the administrator to:

✦ To configure blocking of jailbroken or rooted devices on your system, by navigating to the **Security** submenu

✦ Select **Enable** if you want to block jailbroken or rooted devices

Step 4 – setting up role-based access

XenMobile allows granularity over what type of users and mobile devices you want to manage. In addition, it allows you to set up specific groups of users that will manage the XenMobile server along with specific access rights. This is perfect for setting up specific access rights for desktop administrators and other junior administrators to manage the MDM system. The following screenshot shows how Xenmobile administrators can select different types of differentiated access models:

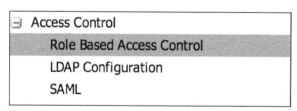

Blocking Jailbroken and Rooted devices

In addition to the role-based access, XenMobile can use LDAP or Microsoft AD to obtain the users or groups that will be managing the system. Administrators always have the option of using built-in users and groups to manage XenMobile as well. To use AD, open the LDAP Configuration window and add in your AD credentials, as shown in the following screenshot:

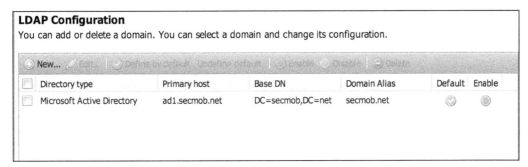

Configuring AD

Step 5 – e-mail configurations

Many of the advanced features require XenMobile to be configured to be able to relay an e-mail from an e-mail server. The e-mail server must be configured to accept SMTP from XenMobile and forward e-mails to external receipts on behalf of XenMobile.

E-mail settings are configured under the **Notification Server** options, as shown in the following screenshot:

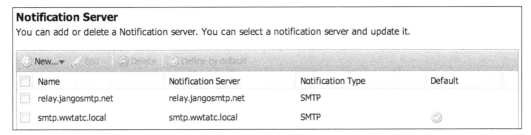

XenMobile SMTP Configuration

Select a new server to configure the SMTP server. XenMobile can use open relay servers or servers that require explicit authentication. If you are using an open relay server, be sure to check the **No Authentication** option. The options for setting up the SMTP server are shown in the following screenshot:

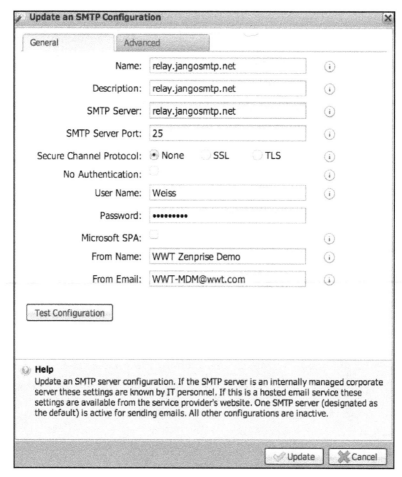

SMTP options

Step 6 – enrolling a mobile device

As we have completed selecting and configuring the options, we may now click on the **Save** button at the bottom of the screen.

Congratulations! You are ready to start enrolling devices, configuring policies, and using the advanced features of XenMobile. Now, we will look at all these aspects and start to embed XenMobile in our organization.

XenMobile allows administrators to enroll devices in numerous ways. The most common way to enroll devices are: sending the user an e-mail, sending a user an SMS link, allowing the user to download the enrollment application, or importing a CSV file for bulk enrollment. All the enrollment options can be found by clicking on the **Enrollment** tab on the main dashboard, as shown in the following screenshot:

Enrolling options

When administrators enroll devices, they will typically start off creating templates for e-mails and text messages. This allows administrators to set custom messages to users. Specific users or groups of users from a local database or an active directory can enroll devices. We can examine the enrollment options, as shown in the following screenshot:

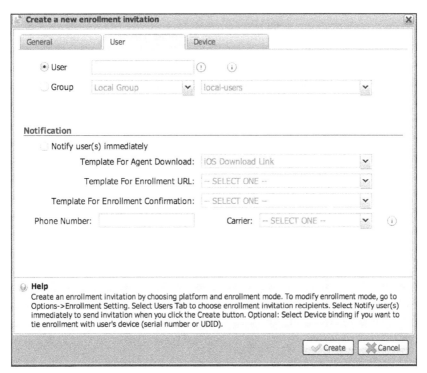

Enrolling devices

Lastly, it is possible that an administrator wants to enroll multiple devices at the same time. They can do this using the bulk import tool by importing a formatted CSV file. The CSV file will allow administrators to import multiple devices for multiple users and categorize them as personal or corporate devices. When XenMobile parses through the CSV file, it will send out an e-mail or text message to the user giving them further instructions on how to complete the enrollment. In the following screenshot, we can see the option to input a **CSV File** into XenMobile:

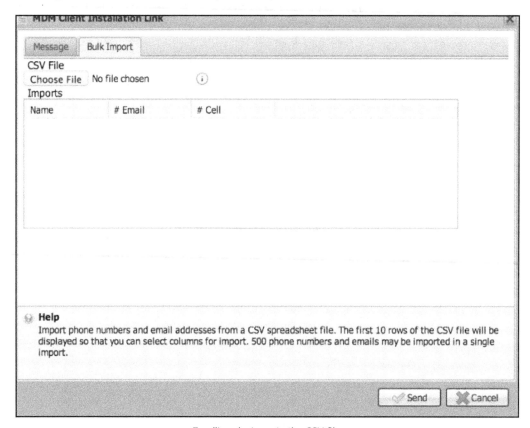

Enrolling devices via the CSV file

Step 7 – configuring a passcode policy

Most mobile security policies require a passcode to be set on the device. The first policy which we will create is to set a passcode, by performing the following steps:

1. Navigate to **Policies | iOS | Configurations**. (we are selecting **iOS** but you can apply these steps to any mobile OS).

2. Navigate to **New Configurations | Profiles and Settings | Passcodes**. We can see the passcode option, along with other configuration options that are available to us in the following screenshot:

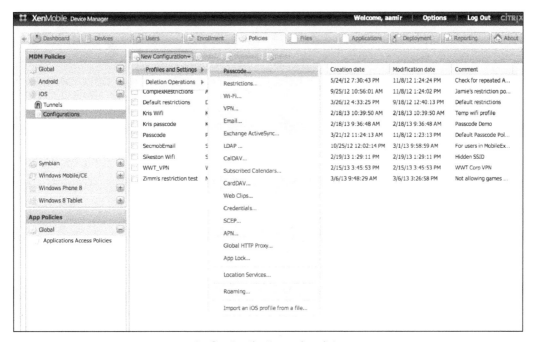

Configuring the Passcode policies

3. Select **Passcode...** and create a custom name for this policy.

4. Click on the **Policy** tab and configure the passcode policy options. The following screenshot shows us the passcode policy options, which we can set as a Xenmobile administrator:

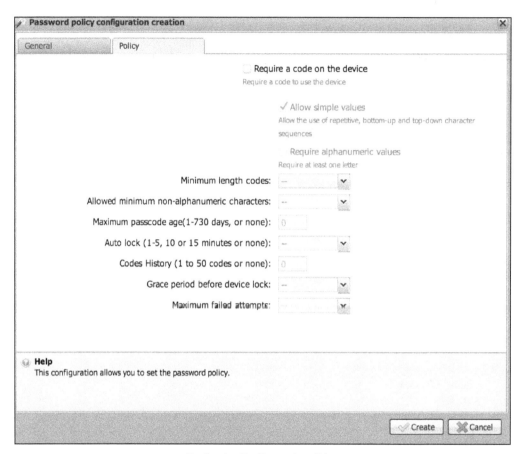

Configuring the Passcode policies

Step 8 – restriction-based policies

iOS restrictions enable administrators of XenMobile to control features for voice dialing and camera usage, limiting Siri usage, YouTube, document syncing to iCloud, and other iOS specific features. Some features only work with the latest version of iOS. In addition, there are features that work with using the Apple Configurator.

Most mobile security policies require a passcode to be set on the device. The next policy we will create is to set a passcode.

1. Navigate to **Policies | iOS | Configurations**. (we are selecting iOS but you can apply these steps to any mobile OS)

2. Select **Restrictions**. The following screenshot shows iOS restrictions. The restriction options are specific to the selected OS and also show the applicable features for the selected OS:

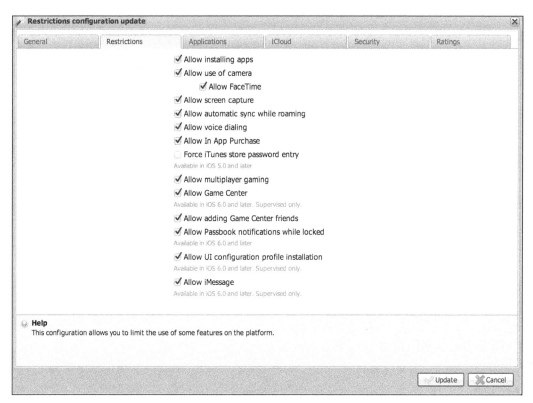

iOS restrictions

iCloud restrictions specifically manage if data can be stored on iCloud. Apple uses iCloud to store data, documents, and photos. Photos on iCloud can be streamed across multiple devices for a user. Many corporations want to ensure that data is not being backed up to a user's personal cloud service. iOS restrictions can manage cloud storage options for iCloud. If a XenMobile adminstrator is concerned about other cloud storage platforms such as Dropbox and Box.net, they need to implement application specific policies (if available) for those specific applications. The iOS restrictions are currently only compatible with Apple's iCloud offering, and not with any third-party solutions. The following screenshot depicts iOS **iCloud** restrictions, which the XenMobile administrators can configure for their organization:

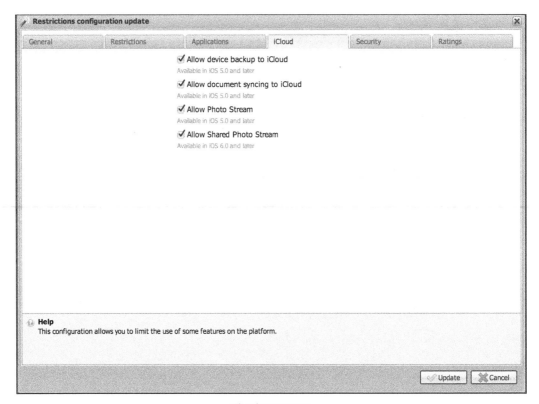

iCloud restrictions

Apple devices, by default, allow the user to accept and trust unsigned certificates or connections to untrusted servers. If you are a corporation and have your own data servers, you need to inform the Apple devices to trust your server. Therefore, Apple gives the ability to trust third-party certificates. Attackers also use third-party certificates to gain access to mobile platforms. They do this by tricking users into browsing to websites on their mobile phones or having them connect to rogue wireless networks. Therefore, some organizations may want to restrict non-trusted HTTPS prompts and only allow access to trusted sites.

In addition, administrators have the option of disabling JavaScript in the web browser, potentially reducing the likelihood of Java-based exploits. The security and web restrictions policies that can be configured on iOS devices are shown in the following screenshot:

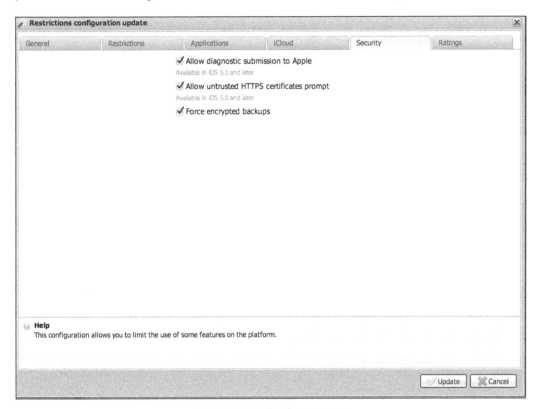

The Security and web Restrictions

Step 9 – Android Samsung SAFE restrictions

Most of the Android devices offer a small subset of restrictions as compared to Apple devices. Android devices also have limited methods for enforcing restrictions. One notable exception is Samsung devices, which offer more granular restrictions than most other Android devices when they are using the Samsung Android **SAFE** (**Samsung Android for Enterprises**) architecture. Samsung SAFE gives administrators the ability to provide access to specific built-in applications, hardware restrictions on camera, and wireless settings. In addition, using the SAFE architecture we can manage and restrict over-the-air upgrades: factory reset options, voice dialing, and screenshot captures.

Samsung SAFE allows administrators to provide restrictions on how much data a particular device should use and take action after a predetermined threshold has been met. Restrictions based on network access can come in handy when corporations are being charged for data. XenMobile can help administrators using Samsung devices to properly manage the device data. The following screenshot shows the data and network restrictions that can be configured by XenMobile administrators using the Samsung SAFE architecture:

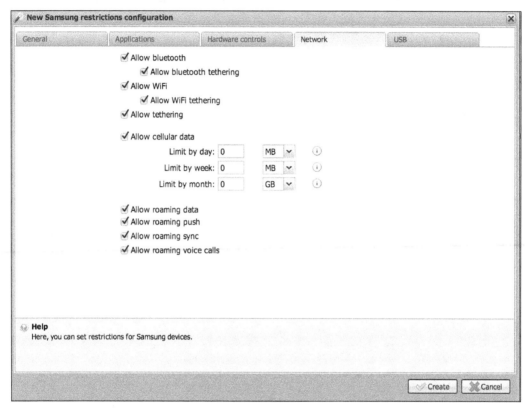

Samsung SAFE Restrictions

Step 10 – deploying and activating a policy

Most mobile security policies require a passcode to be set on the device. Passcode policies enable encryption on devices and secure transactions such as mobile payment through NFC and certificates. We will create the next policy, by performing the following steps:

1. Navigate to **Deployment | iOS Base Package | Edit**.

2. Select **Edit**. We will edit a base package and add a passcode policy, as shown in the following screenshot:

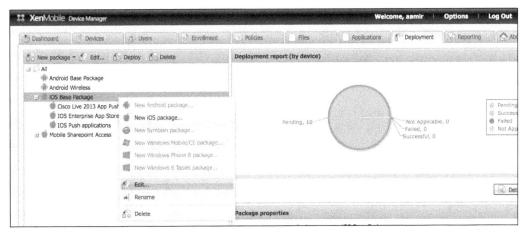

Deploying a Policy

3. Select **Group of Users**. Select the users you want the policy to be applied to.

4. Select **Resources**. Add your passcode policy from the available resource pool to the deployment pool.

5. Select and configure any additional resources you may want to deploy.

6. Click on **Finish**.

You have now configured XenMobile, set up server options, enrolled devices, and configured basic policies. In the next section, we will discuss the top features of XenMobile and learn how we can use these features to embed mobile devices into our organization in an efficient and secured manner.

Top 6 features you need to know about

As you start to use XenMobile, you will realize that there is a wide variety of things that you can do with it. This section will teach you all about the most commonly performed tasks and most commonly used features in XenMobile.

Reporting

XenMobile has one of the most important features of reporting the modules available in the mobile device manager software packages. Reporting gives XenMobile administrators a way to track devices, features, and violations in a mobile policy.

The process to access the reporting module is as follows:

1. Log in to your XenMobile server (`http://server_ip_address/zdm`).

The login screen

2. XenMobile has numerous reporting options that can be used to track the status of mobile devices, installed applications, and policy compliance. Click on the **Reporting** tab to see the reporting screen, as shown in the following screenshot:

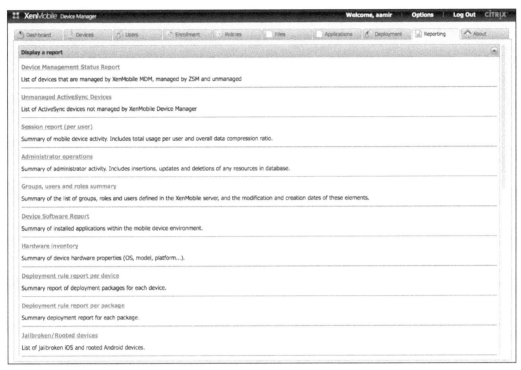

Reports

3. Select a report.

There are many reports, which you will find interesting. Most of them are self-explanatory. For example, hardware inventory will give you a breakdown of devices, OS, and models. Other reports that are popular are for jailbroken devices and rooted devices that show possible violations of default security settings, which could make the device vulnerable to external attacks. Overall, the reporting section will be used to review the current state of mobile devices in your organization. The following screenshot shows an example of types of devices in an organization by OS and platform (these reports can be exported into the PDF format):

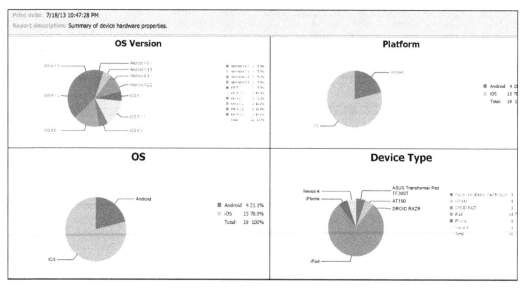

Reports

Application stores

If you have internally developed iOS apps (. ipa or any iOS apps that you have licensed to distribute, you can upload those apps directly to the device manager database and deploy those apps to users' devices. XenMobile allows administrators to distribute applications to users by allowing an organization to run its own internal application stores. In addition, XenMobile allows administrators to install on or remove the applications from Google and Apple devices via the push method. The push method is an automatic installation or removal of applications to the mobile device without the need for the user to go to an application store to install an application, or manually deleting an application. The installation process is as follows:

1. Log in to your XenMobile server at `http://server_ip_address/zdm`.

2. Click on the **Application** tab.

3. Navigate to **New | New App**.

4. You have a few options here, which you can select. They are as follows:

  ○ **Push Remove Application**: This option removes the installed application
  ○ **Do not backup**: This option will not back up an application or application data

5. Install the application via push or make it available via the internal Enterprise AppStore.
6. Install **External Apps** from AppStore.

You will now be able to install and manage applications on mobile devices in your organization, as shown in the following screenshot. The following screenshot displays the XenMobile's application store. The table shown in the following screenshot displays applications for every platform. At the time of writing this book, we couldn't filter this view to show only applications for specific platforms:

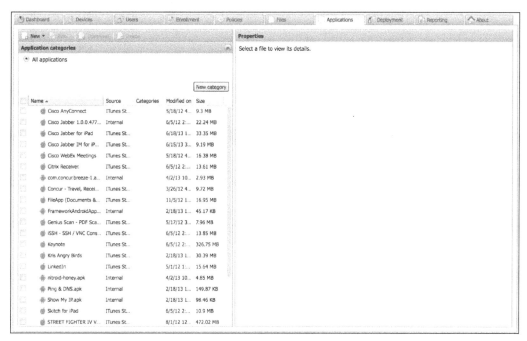

The Application store

Xenmobile provides you the unique ability to import your own applications, or link to an AppStore application for iOS devices. Lastly, you have the ability to add a **volume purchase program** (**VPP**) license file. A VPP license file allows an organization to purchase a bulk set of licenses of a single application. Therefore, their users do not have to download the same application and pay for it individually. Currently, VPP is only available for iOS applications of Apple platforms.

Secure Mail Gateway

Secure Mobile Gateway provides granular access control for e-mail and calendar applications on devices that support Microsoft ActiveSync. You can configure Secure Mobile Gateway to allow or block access to Microsoft Exchange servers from mobile devices based on numerous device characteristics. They include the ownership of the devices, installed applications, devices rooted or jailbroken status, applications installed, and other conditions. When a device is blocked or allowed, it is reported on the XenMobile ZDM dashboard, so that the administrators have one unified view of the status of the devices.

The benefit of Secure Mobile Gateway is that it ensures that a user won't bypass your XenMobile policies that are being enforced on devices. A user who does not agree with your policies may decide to skip enrollment. He may have somehow decided that he does not need corporate applications that are being pushed or other device centric policies. However, typically most users will need access to their e-mail from their devices. If a user somehow figures out the necessary settings and credentials to configure his device manually, Secure Mobile Gateway can intercept that connection and make policies decisions based on an organization's needs. In other words, you could stop a user from accessing e-mails until he enrolls in the XenMobile MDM solution.

XenMobile Secure Mobile Gateway provides access to controls of SSL (HTTPS) ActiveSync requests made by mobile devices against backend exchange **Client Access Servers** (**CAS**).

Secure Mobile Gateway uses rules to allow or block access. A device client request is evaluated against the organization's polices. XenMobile Secure Mobile Gateway will make the determination if the mobile device is allowed to connect with the organization's Microsoft Exchange server. Xenmobile will then determine whether to allow or block access to the e-mail server from the mobile device based on the mobile device's status and the organization's security policy.

You can also use Secure Mobile Gateway to encrypt e-mail attachments that pass through the Exchange server, to ensure that only users with approved managed devices can view company documents securely and safely on their devices.

To install Secure Mobile Gateway on Windows 2008 servers you must perform the following steps:

1. Configure the Microsoft Forefront Threat Management Gateway.

2. Install Citrix Secure Mobile Gateway on the server running Microsoft Forefront Threat Management Gateway as an ISAPI plugin.

3. Use the Citrix SMG Installer application that came with your software.

4. Once Secure Mobile Gateway is installed, you can configure the instructions of Secure Mobile Gateway under the XenMobile server options.

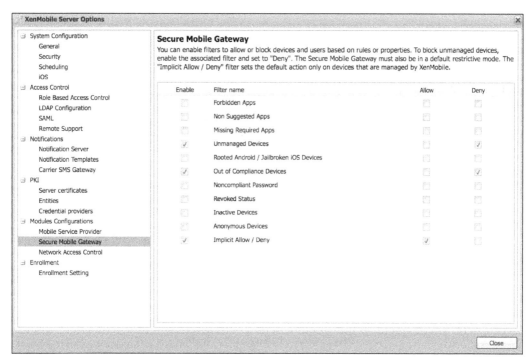

Secure Mobile Gateway Options

We gave some basic highlights on how to install Secure Mobile Gateway. It should be noted that the installation of the Secure Mobile Gateway requires the administrator to have access on the Exchange environment to install the software. Additionally, Citrix's XenMobile documentation should be referred to for updates or changes. The following screenshot outlines how the administrators can quickly manage and view the status of the devices managed via Secure Mobile Gateway:

	Jailbro...	SMG...	Manag...	Serial number	IMEI/MEID	First co...	Last aut...	User	OS	Inac...	Status	Model	Platf...	OS v...
				028040434460E1D7		10/3/12...	10/3/12...	cries@s...		288 ...	Inac...	AT100	Andr...	4.0.4
				353918058425808	35391805842...	2/20/13...	6/29/13...	anonym...		19 d...	Inac...	Nexus 4	Andr...	4.2.2
				99000121261026	99000121261...	4/29/13...	7/18/13...	cchaffee...		0 day	Active	DROID...	Andr...	4.1.2
				C4OKCT163059		10/19/1...	10/19/1...	brobins...		272 ...	Inac...	ASUS T...	Andr...	4.1.1
				DLXFFX4KDFJ2	01 266900 12...	5/25/12...	4/19/13...	anonym...		90 d...	Inac...	iPad	iOS	6.0.1
				DLXGVJRDDKNW	01 293000 43...	2/18/13...	3/20/13...	kgarner...		120 ...	Inac...	iPad	iOS	6.1.2
				DLXH95YRDJ8T		8/16/12...	8/31/12...	nbogan...		321 ...	Inac...	iPad	iOS	5.1.1
				DLXH9C4EDVGJ	01 311600 06...	4/26/12...	8/7/12 ...	kbomar...		345 ...	Inac...	iPad	iOS	5.1.1
				DLXH9PQVDJ8T		6/1/12 ...	3/25/13...	anonym...		115 ...	Inac...	iPad	iOS	6.1.2
				DMQJM4MNF182		3/22/13...	3/22/13...	cchaffee...		118 ...	Inac...			
				DMQKH9V1F182		6/18/13...	7/10/13...	wwtlive1		8 days	Inac...	iPad	iOS	6.1.3
				DMRG7T6SDFHW		5/24/12...	10/23/1...	ladefala...		268 ...	Inac...	iPad	iOS	5.1.1
				DMRJJ5ARF185		2/14/13...	3/28/13...	alakhani...		112 ...	Inac...	iPad	iOS	6.1.2
				DMTJJPLFF182		12/12/1...	1/2/13 ...	bortbals...		197 ...	Inac...	iPad	iOS	6.0.1
				DN6G7VTZDFJ2	01 292700 09...	8/28/12...	8/28/12...	ladefala...		324 ...	Inac...	iPad	iOS	5.1.1
				DN6GLK92DFHY		6/18/13...	7/18/13...	tim		0 day	Active	iPad	iOS	6.1.3
				DN6GVZPSDFHY		5/1/12 ...	3/21/13...	bortbals...		119 ...	Inac...	iPad	iOS	6.1.2
				DQTFQ24TDFHW		5/29/12...	10/25/1...	hoelzer...		266 ...	Inac...	iPad	iOS	5.1
				DQTFQ28WDFHW		5/16/12...	9/21/12...	bortbals...		300 ...	Inac...	iPad	iOS	5.1.1
				DR5J27J9DFHW		9/23/12...	3/30/13...	mzimme...		110 ...	Inac...	iPad	iOS	6.0.1
				DYTHN1XVDVGF	99000096402...	5/27/12...	3/23/13...	anonym...		117 ...	Inac...	iPad	iOS	6.1.2
				DYVHQQ21DJ8T		6/18/12...	12/10/1...	waltersd...		220 ...	Inac...	iPad	iOS	6.0
				QR227B4ZA4S	01 312600 58...	10/17/1...	3/22/13...	adiwaka...		118 ...	Inac...	iPhone	iOS	5.1.1

Device Status when managed via SMG

The XenMobile service manager

The XenMobile service manager, or commonly referred to as ZSM is an add-on for Blackberry environments. It requires the installation of Blackberry Enterprise Server (in most cases). It allows XenMobile to access Blackberry services and remotely manage, lock, and wipe Blackberry devices. Please note, that ZSM is normally used to manage Blackberry devices prior to version 10 of Blackberry OS. Most Blackberry devices running Blackberry OS 10 can communicate directly with ActiveSync. However, Blackberry OS 10 can still be managed via Blackberry Enterprise Servers, and in those cases it can still be used with ZSM.

To use ZSM, simply install the ZSM file onto the Blackberry device you plan to manage. You may need to complete additional steps on your Blackberry Enterprise Server that are dependent on your specific business configuration.

Dashboard management

Citrix XenMobile MDM Dashboard is a way to have a quick view of the status of the current system. The dashboard can be customized by using different graphs and charts that open up based on the settings for the user authenticating the system. The following screenshot is an example of the XenMobile dashboard:

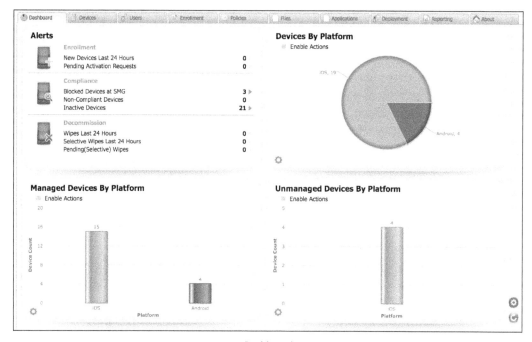

Dashboard

The dashboard's **Alerts** section gives an administrator the option to monitor the following alerts:

✦ New enrollments

✦ Non compliance

✦ Inactive devices

✦ Secure Mobile Gateway blocked users

✦ Device wipes (completed, full, selective, and pending)

The following screenshot shows the current alerts for recent events:

Alerts

	Enrollment	
	New Devices Last 24 Hours	**0**
	Pending Activation Requests	**0**
	Compliance	
	Blocked Devices at SMG	**3** ▶
	Non-Compliant Devices	**0**
	Inactive Devices	**21** ▶
	Decommission	
	Wipes Last 24 Hours	**0**
	Selective Wipes Last 24 Hours	**0**
	Pending(Selective) Wipes	**0**

Alert Status

Additional alerts that can be configured on the Dashboard include:

✦ **Device Actions**: It is an embedded dashboard widget that lets administrators interact with multiple devices and send alerts and messages to those devices.

✦ **Charts**: It allows administrators to view mobile devices and group devices in multiple views. In addition, charts lets an administrator group devices by their functionality in an organization, such as employee owned or BYOD devices, as well as other categories. It is a great tool for administrators to quickly gain an understanding of devices on their network, as well as to categorize and compare other devices they have in their organization. For example, charts may be used by administrators to compare how many iPhones have been updated to the latest iOS software and how many are running older firmware. The following are the other device categories:

  ○ **Devices by platform**: This displays BYOD devices by their operating system, such as iOS, Blackberry, or Android.

  ○ **Managed devices by platform**: This displays BYOD and corporate managed devices by their operating system, such as iOS, Blackberry, or Android.

  ○ **Unmanaged devices by platform**: This option displays devices that were previously managed by XenMobile, but are no longer managed by the system, nor do they have corporate certificates. The reason these devices fall into this category is because they were previously managed but now have been wiped.

- ° **Device by Secure Mobile Gateway status**: This option gives administrators status of the devices that have interacted with Secure Mobile Gateway. This option will allow administrators to view what devices have been managed or blocked by Secure Mobile Gateway.

- ° **Devices blocked by reason**: This option allows administrators to view all the devices that are blocked. This option breaks down for administrators why devices are blocked and how many devices have violated a security policy, or do not have access to corporate resources. Some examples are the devices blocked because they fail a security policy, have blacklisted applications or invalid certificates that can be categorized and viewed by administrators.

- ° **Device ownership**: This option allows administrators to view all the devices and verify if they are corporate managed devices or BYOD devices.

- ° **Android Touchdown license status**: This option displays the status of touchdown licenses on Android devices.

- ° **Failed package deployments**: These options will allow administrators to view what packages or applications have failed to install on mobile devices and which devices they failed to install on.

Citrix XenMobile MDM **Dashboard** gives administrators the power to customize the dashboard which we explored earlier. Each administrator's dashboard is customized to their own view and setup. The following screenshot is an example of a dashboard that has been customized with the options that were discussed in this section:

A customized Dashboard by different administrators

Common management tasks

Citrix XenMobile MDM **Dashboard** gives administrators a quick way to handle common management tasks related to XenMobile. In the following example, we will examine how administrators can perform actions on a device from the dashboard, by performing the following steps:

1. Click on the **Devices** tab.

2. Select the device you want to perform a task on and right-click on the device:

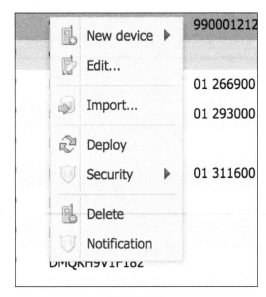

Alert Status

Now that we know how to quickly access the menu to perform device actions, let's examine what security options are available.

3. Select the **Security** menu.

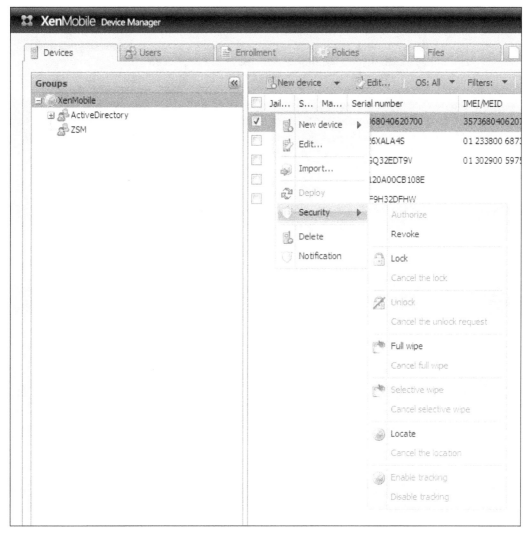

Alert Status

The **Security** menu allows us to perform the following options:

✦ **Lock**: Administrators can lock devices from this screen. If a passcode exists on a device, it will be required to unlock it.

✦ **Selective Wipe**: This option will wipe all the corporate and managed data. The user's personal data, applications, and pictures will be left intact on the device.

✦ **Full Wipe**: This option will completely wipe the devices and then the devices will be reset to default factory settings.

◆ **Locate**: This option determines the location of the device using cellular tower triangulation and, if available, GPS. The results will be displayed on a map. It is important to note that this feature is highly dependent on the device's settings and capabilities. Furthermore, administrators may have legal restrictions on how they track and locate people in their organization.

We just explained the top features in Citrix XenMobile. XenMobile has over 300 features and within the context of this book we cannot cover all of them. However, the features we covered are the most popular and widely used. In the next section, we will cover people and places you should get to know that will familiarize you with some of the resources which will help you in learning more about the other features available in XenMobile and start implementing them in your organization.

People and places you should get to know

If you need help with Citrix XenMobile MDM, here are some people and places which will prove very useful.

Official sites

✦ Homepage: http://www.citrix.com/products/xenmobile/overview.html

✦ Manual and documentation: http://support.citrix.com/proddocs/topic/cloudgateway/xmob-mdm-landing-page-con.html

Articles and tutorials

The following are some of the tutorials on how to get started with XenMobile:

✦ A six minute video from NunoQueirosAlves on an overview of XenMobile MDM is found at http://www.youtube.com/watch?v=d75qHTkVRuE

✦ An official video from Citrix on how to integrate XenMobile into the enterprise (this is a 46 minute video which will give you an in-depth, advanced look at many features associated with the product) is found at http://www.youtube.com/watch?v=o4vQ6lNXx9E

✦ A video that highlights how to enroll mobile devices with XenMobile is found at http://www.youtube.com/watch?v=U0cl9Z6DLZg

Community

✦ **Official mailing list**: It is the XenMobile's mailing list, which has been replaced by forums

✦ **Official forums**: http://forums.citrix.com/category.jspa?categoryID=302

✦ **User FAQ**: Refer to the official forums. Product marketing FAQ can be found at http://www.citrix.com/products/xenmobile/features/mdm.html

✦ **World wide technology**: It provides expert mobile professional services to install and implement XenMobile at http://www.wwt.com

Blogs

The following are the influential blogs on XenMobile products:

- ✦ Dr. Chaos (dark security and total chaos) is a resource for mobile security and BYOD found at `http://www.drchaos.com/`
- ✦ The official Citrix mobility blog is found at `http://blogs.citrix.com/tag/xenmobile/`
- ✦ World wide technology's official blog is found at `https://www2.wwt.com/blogs`

Twitter

- ✦ Follow the official XenMobile's Twitter account at `https://twitter.com/XenMobile`
- ✦ Follow Dr. Chaos, the author of this book at `https://twitter.com/aamirlakhani`
- ✦ Follow Aman Diwakar, the Cyber expert at `https://twitter.com/DDOS`
- ✦ For more open source information, follow Packt at `http://twitter.com/#!/packtopensource`

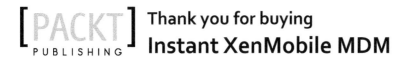

Thank you for buying
Instant XenMobile MDM

About Packt Publishing

Packt, pronounced 'packed', published its first book "*Mastering phpMyAdmin for Effective MySQL Management*" in April 2004 and subsequently continued to specialize in publishing highly focused books on specific technologies and solutions.

Our books and publications share the experiences of your fellow IT professionals in adapting and customizing today's systems, applications, and frameworks. Our solution based books give you the knowledge and power to customize the software and technologies you're using to get the job done. Packt books are more specific and less general than the IT books you have seen in the past. Our unique business model allows us to bring you more focused information, giving you more of what you need to know, and less of what you don't.

Packt is a modern, yet unique publishing company, which focuses on producing quality, cutting-edge books for communities of developers, administrators, and newbies alike. For more information, please visit our website: www.packtpub.com.

Writing for Packt

We welcome all inquiries from people who are interested in authoring. Book proposals should be sent to author@packtpub.com. If your book idea is still at an early stage and you would like to discuss it first before writing a formal book proposal, contact us; one of our commissioning editors will get in touch with you.

We're not just looking for published authors; if you have strong technical skills but no writing experience, our experienced editors can help you develop a writing career, or simply get some additional reward for your expertise.

PhoneGap 2.x Mobile Application Development Hotshot

ISBN: 978-1-84951-940-3   Paperback: 388 pages

Create exciting apps for mobile devices using PhoneGap

1. Ten apps included to help you get started on your very own exciting mobile app

2. These apps include working with localization, social networks, geolocation, as well as the camera, audio, video, plugins, and more

3. Apps cover the spectrum from productivity apps, educational apps, all the way to entertainment and games

4. Explore design patterns common in apps designed for mobile devices

Netduino Home Automation Projects

ISBN: 978-1-84969-782-8   Paperback: 108 pages

Automate your house, save lives, and survive the apocalypse with .NET on a Netduino!

1. Automate your house using a Netduino and a bunch of common components

2. Learn the fundamentals of Netduino to implement them in almost any project

3. Create cool projects ranging from self-watering plants to a homemade breathalyzer

Please check **www.PacktPub.com** for information on our titles

Creating Mobile Apps with jQuery Mobile

ISBN: 978-1-78216-006-9   Paperback: 254 pages

Learn to make practical, unique, real-world sites that span a variety of industries and technologies with the world's most popular mobile development library

1. Write less, do more: learn to apply the jQuery motto to quickly craft creative sites that work on any smartphone and even not-so-smart phones

2. Learn to leverage HTML5 audio and video, geolocation, Twitter, Flickr, blogs, Reddit, Google maps, content management system, and much more

3. All examples are either in use in the real world or were used as examples to win business across several industries

Instant PrimeFaces Starter [Instant]

ISBN: 978-1-84951-990-8   Paperback: 90 pages

Design and develop awesome web user interfaces for desktop and mobile devices with PrimeFaces and JSF2 using practical, hands-on examples

1. Learn something new in an Instant! A short, fast, focused guide delivering immediate results

2. Integrate Google Maps in your web application to show search results with markers and overlays with the PrimeFaces gmap component

3. Develop a customizable dashboard for your users that displays charts with live data, news feeds, and draggable widgets

4. Implement a live chat system that uses Prime Push to send updates to desktop and mobile users simultaneously

Please check **www.PacktPub.com** for information on our titles

www.ingramcontent.com/pod-product-compliance
Lightning Source LLC
LaVergne TN
LVHW080105070326

832902LV00014B/2432

* 9 7 8 1 8 4 9 6 9 6 2 6 5 *